MACHINES RULE!

IN AN EMERGENCY

Steve Parker

W
FRANKLIN WATTS

First published in 2008
by Franklin Watts

Franklin Watts
338 Euston Road
London NW1 3BH

Franklin Watts Australia
Level 17/207 Kent Street
Sydney, NSW 2000

Editor: Jeremy Smith
Design: Billin Design Solutions
Art director: Jonathan Hair

Picture credits: Alan Novelli/Alamy: 3,
6, 11c, 21t. Ashley Cooper/Alamy: 21
tr and br. Corbis: 10. Chuck
Pefley/Alamy: 25b. Dominic
Burke/Alamy: 23br. Imagepix/Alamy:
8t. Jack Sullivan/Alamy: 16, 23tl.
Powered by Light/Alan Spencer/Alamy:
19. SHOUT/Alamy: 19b.
Stockfolio/Alamy: 26, 27b.
Tom Wood/Alamy: 19c.

A CIP catalogue record for this book
is available from the British Library.

Dewey number:629.225

ISBN 978 0 7496 7932 3

Printed in China

Franklin Watts is a division of
Hachette Children's Books,
an Hachette Livre UK company.

CONTENTS

Emergency! Let's go!

Accident, illness and disaster can happen anywhere, any time. That's when the emergency services spring into action. Police, paramedics, firefighters and lifeboat crews rush to the scene, to save lives and help victims in need of many different types of help.

Air emergencies

If you get in trouble in a place that is hard to reach, sometimes you need to be rescued by air. Natural disasters can be fought from above too. Special planes can drop water from the sky to put out raging forest fires.

Firefighting

Flames, smoke, fumes, poison gases, explosive chemicals, collapsing buildings, crashed cars – all these emergencies and more require the help of the fire service.

Rescue at sea

If you are stuck at sea, you depend on a lifeboat crew to rescue you. These men and women are trained volunteers, and have other jobs when they are not on the lifeboats.

Police and ambulance

If a crime or traffic accident happens, dial '999' and police will speed to the scene to help out. Call the same number for an ambulance in the event of an accident.

Ambulance

Ambulances save thousands of lives every year. They speed to a huge range of emergency scenes, from road accidents and buildings on fire to seriously ill people in need of urgent medical help.

An ambulance sounds its siren as it races to an urgent call or 'shout'. The crews are trained **paramedics** and also excellent drivers.

7091

Estate cars can also be used for ambulance work.

AMBULANCE SERVICE

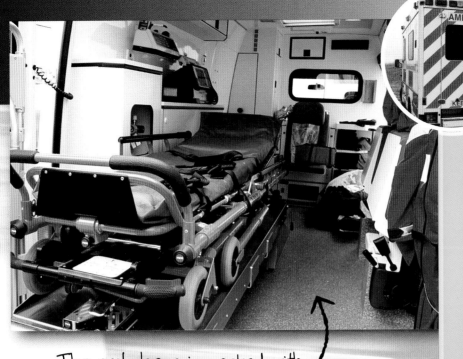

The ambulance is packed with life-saving equipment.

Iveco Daily City Van, Ambulance Version (below)

Length: 5.47 metres

Width: 1.99 metres

Height: 2.63 metres

Weight: Up to 4 tonnes

Interior maximum width: 1.8 metres

Interior maximum length: 2.6 metres

Interior maximum height: 1.9 metres

Engine: 2.8 litres turbo diesel

Power: 146 horsepower

THAT'S INCREDIBLE

In Britain, someone has a heart attack every two minutes. Thousands of people are saved by ambulance crew and their equipment.

Back at the hospital or medical centre, ambulances are checked and restocked with supplies, ready for the next call.

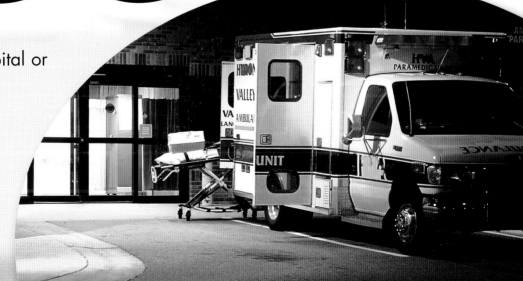

Fire engine

Fire engines or appliances come in many shapes and sizes. Sometimes they are called out to tackle blazes, but other times they are used to rescue people from crashed vehicles, dangerous buildings, tall trees and deep holes.

THAT'S INCREDIBLE

The London Fire Brigade has more than 240 ordinary fire engines, 30 aerial ladder platforms (ALP), five fire investigation units and two fireboats!

Crew aboard, the fire engine sets off on an emergency 'shout'. They are in constant touch by radio with their station and the other emergency services.

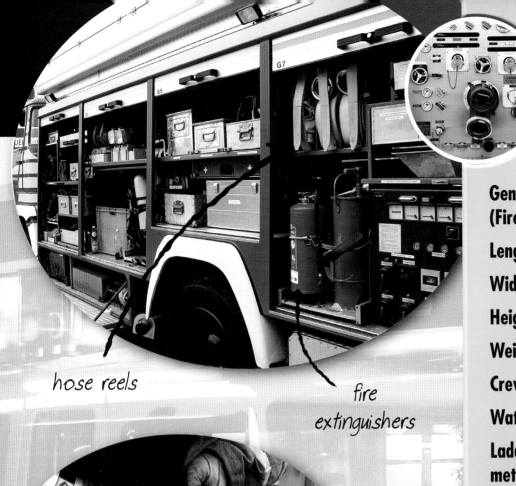

hose reels

fire extinguishers

Stats and Facts

General Fire Appliance (Fire Engine)

Length: 7.7 metres

Width: 2.33 metres

Height: 3.2 metres

Weight: 11.2 tonnes

Crew: 5

Water capacity: 1,365 litres

Ladders: 13.5 metres and 9 metres extending

Hoses: 8 lengths of hose 18 metres long and 7 centimetres wide, 4 lengths of hose 25 metres long and 4.5 centimetres wide

Metal cutter/spreaders have powerful jaws

The fire engine carries some water and foam. But when the crew arrives at the scene of a fire, they look for a mains water connection or **hydrant** to feed water to the fire engine.

Aerial ladder platform

If you want to aim high, you need an aerial ladder platform (ALP). It can save people from tall buildings, carry a water hose to spray down on a fire, and even rescue a frightened kitten in a tree.

Hydraulic (piston-operated) 'legs' keep the vehicle stable when the ladder is extended.

Stats and Facts

The boom operator works levers which extend the ladder, raise its angle of tilt, swivel the rotating turntable, and work the water spray.

Scania/Bronto Skylift

F30 HDT ALP

Platform height: 28 metres

Water output: 2,300 litres per minute

Engine: Scania 11 litre intercooled turbo diesel

Power: 320 horsepower

Gears: Allison 5 speed fully automatic gearbox

Crew: 4 basic, up to 7

Special features: ABS antilock braking, CCTV security, foam sprayer, radio link to cage

THAT'S INCREDIBLE
The highest turntable ladder platforms reach to the 15th floor, and computer controls stop them swaying.

The ladder has several sections that slide out like a telescope, mounted on a turntable. The top cage forms an aerial firefighting platform, with water pumped up from the vehicle below.

Police cars

Crash, crime, crisis, catastrophe – the police arrive in minutes. They rely on expert driving, instant information on the radio, and a souped-up car packed with the latest gadgets and equipment.

With siren wailing and lights flashing, everyone has to make way for the 'cop car'. It is the police who organise the other emergency services.

THAT'S INCREDIBLE

A police driver reached a speed of 256 km/h (159 mph) as he tried out a new squad car in 2005.

Gallardo

Maker: Lamborghini (Italy)

Length: 4.3 metres

Width: 1.9 metres

Height: 1.16 metres

Engine: 5 litre V10 petrol

Horsepower: 520

Acceleration: 0–100 km/h in 4 seconds

Top speed: 327 km/h

The most important piece of kit in a police car attending an accident scene is a broom – to sweep up rubbish.

The Italians have the fastest police cars – Lamborghini Gallardos. They race to emergencies on the country's main southern highway, and also rush body parts to hospital for medical transplants!

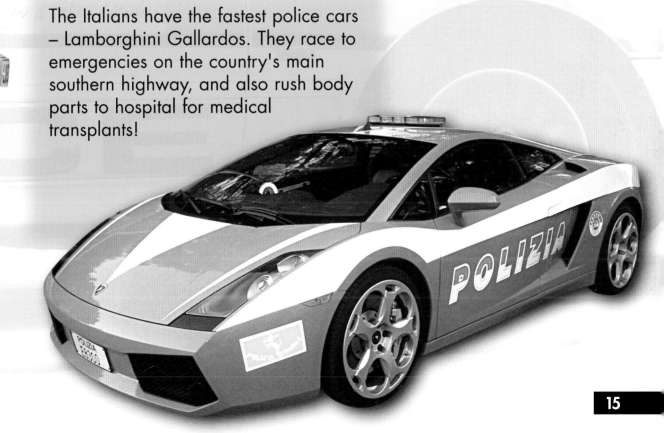

Police motorcycle

At a road emergency, the police motorcycle is usually first to arrive. It zooms along clear roads, weaves through traffic and squeezes between cars. At once the rider contacts base by radio to organize the rescue.

There are many types of police bikes, from the Hondas to BMWs (left) and even Harley-Davidsons in the United States

THAT'S INCREDIBLE

In very cold places, police riders wear special heated suits which they can plug into the motorcycle's electrical system.

Stats and Facts

In Boston, USA, bikes wait outside while their riders receive their daily instructions, or briefing, in the police station.

Honda Pan European ST1100P Police Edition

Length: 2.28 metres

Wheelbase: 1.55 metres

Width: 0.93 metres including panniers

Height: 1.40 metres

Weight: 327 kilograms

Fuel tank: 28 litres

Top speed: 230 km/h

Engine: 1.08 litres Longitudinal V4

Gears: 5 speed

Police riders have a **microphone** and headphones built into their helmets.

Air ambulance

If the roads are blocked, the fields are flooded and the bridges are down, it is time to call the air ambulance helicopter. With a small patch of ground to land, no emergency vehicle is faster than this life-saver.

A major road accident causes massive traffic jams. But the air ambulance flies in fast, hovers to check all is clear, then touches down safely.

Stars and Facts

Casualties are flown straight to hospital.

Flying a helicopter means controlling several levers and pedals all at once.

American Eurocopter BK117

Length including rotor overhang: 13 metres

Width including rotors: 11 metres

Height: 3.85 metres

Empty weight: 1.92 tonnes

Maximum take-off weight: 3.5 tonnes

Top speed: 260 km/h

Cruising speed: 246 km/h

Engines: 2 Turbomeca Arriel 1E2 turboshafts

THAT'S INCREDIBLE

In Britain a typical air ambulance costs £1 million to run each year. Most depend on money from donations and charities.

A trained doctor checks a casualty as the air ambulance races to the nearest hospital.

Rescue helicopter

Search and Rescue (SAR) helicopters buzz off to any emergency. People get swept out to sea, stuck on a shipwreck, stranded by the tide, fall down cliffs, sink into mud, slip off a boat - and that's just one day's work for the SAR team!

The **SAR** helicopter has to be ready to go at any time. The HH-60 Pave Hawk has an engine/rotor blade anti-ice system so it can fly in even the coldest conditions.

Stats and Facts

rotor blades

As the SAR helicopter arrives, it hovers above the site and checks the weather, wind and the best way to carry out the rescue.

A stretcher with a harness is used to lift people safely onto the helicopter.

HH-60 Pave Hawk

Based on: Sikorsky UH-60 Black Hawk

Length: 17.1 metres

Rotor diameter: 14.1 metres

Height: 5.1 metres

Empty weight: 7.2 tonnes

Maximum take-off weight: 9.9 tonnes

Top speed: 295 km/h

Engines: 2 GE T700-701C turboshafts

Power: 3,200 horsepower

Range: 810 kilometres

THAT'S INCREDIBLE
Some SAR 'choppers' have a hoist cable 60 metres long, which can lift 270 kilograms – the weight of four adults.

The pilot has many modern aids including cameras, **sat nav** and radio contact.

Lifeboat

Few emergencies are as terrifying as a shipwreck, falling overboard or being cast adrift in the ocean. In Britain, the Royal Naval Lifeboat Institution (RNLI) has been saving those in peril on the sea for almost 200 years.

Storms and rough seas are when many people get into distress. The lifeboat and its crew are tough, all-weather rescuers. If the lifeboat is tipped over by a big wave, it turns right way up again at once. This is know as self-righting.

Stats and Facts

Severn Class Lifeboat

Builder: Green Marine

Length: 17 metres

Width: 5.5 metres

Weight: 40 tonnes

Top speed: 45 km/h

Engines: 2 Caterpillar

3412 TA marine diesels

Power: 2,500 horsepower

Crew: 6

Fuel tanks: 5,500 litres

Range: 460 kilometres

Glass panels give a great all-round view.

Some lifeboats slide down a slope into the sea.

THAT'S INCREDIBLE

It costs a lot of money – £300,000 – to keep just one lifeboat running all year. This is paid for by voluntary donations.

Small blow-up lifeboats called Rigid-hulled Inflatable Boats (**RIBs**) are very useful in shallow water. Some big lifeboats carry their own RIBs.

Fireboat

A fireboat is designed to put out fires and deal with other emergencies on boats and ships, on lakes and rivers and seas, on oil rigs, along harbours and docks, at waterfronts and at warehouses.

The fire seems to be out. But the fireboat stands by and 'damps down' to make sure the flames do not flare up again.

Fireboats spray water during celebrations.

THAT'S INCREDIBLE

The Los Angeles Fire Department's Fireboat Number 2 *Warner Lawrence* can pump 144,000 litres of water per minute 120 metres in the air.

Typical Fireboat

Length: 10-30 metres

Width: 4-8 metres

Pumping rate: Up to 140,000 litres per minute

Top speed: 20 km/h

Engines: Twin marine diesels

Power: 800 horsepower

Water pumping power: 800 horsepower

Special features: Water cannons or fire monitors, foam to spray onto burning oil, emergency lighting for night work, casualty room with beds, stretchers and medical equipment

outboard craft

The fireboat's small outboard craft can get right up close to the scene of a blaze.

Superscooper

THAT'S INCREDIBLE

It takes the CL-415 Superscooper just 12 seconds to scoop up its full load of 6,137 litres of water, which is about 75 bathtubs-full!

If fire breaks out in a remote place, the Superscooper is the best emergency aircraft to tackle the problem. This twin-propeller plane scoops up water from a sea or lake and 'bombs' it onto the flames.

Bombardier/Canadair CL-415 Superscooper

Length: 19.8 metres

Wingspan: 28.6 metres

Height: 8.98 metres

Empty weight: 11.8 tonnes

Maximum take-off weight: 17.1 tonnes

Top speed: 375 km/h

Cruising speed: 287 km/h

Engines: 2 Pratt & Whitney Canada PW 123 AF turboprops

Crew: 2

Superscoopers are called in where the land is rocky, remote and dry. Even if ordinary fire engines could get to these places, they wouldn't be able to find enough water to spray at the fire.

The pilot prepares to fly through the dense smoke and release the water at exactly the right time to put the fire out.

Glossary

Air ambulance
An emergency vehicle with medical equipment and staff, that is also an aircraft – usually a helicopter or small plane.

ALP
Aerial Ladder Platform, an emergency vehicle carrying a very long extending ladder on a swivelling turntable.

Fire appliance
A 'fire engine', a vehicle that deals with some feature of a fire, such as putting it out with foam or water hoses, or carrying a long ladder.

Fire extinguisher
A device for putting out flames, which usually sprays foam, powder, a gas such as carbon dioxide, or a similar chemical.

Hydrant
A large tap-like connection to the main water pipe in a street or building, for emergency water supplies such as fighting fire.

Hydraulic
Working by the force of high-pressure liquid, usually water or a special oil.

Microphone
A device that turns sound waves into electrical messages, which can then be sent along wires or turned into radio signals.

Outboard
Outside of the main hull of a boat, such as an outboard engine or motor.

Paramedic
A person trained in emergency medical skills, especially in saving life and urgent treatments.

RIB
Rigid-hulled Inflatable Boat, a small boat usually with a solid base and frame and blow-up front and sides.

RNLI
Royal Naval Lifeboat Institution, the organization that fund-raises, buys, operates and maintains lifeboats and their crews, in and around British waters.

SAR
Search And Rescue, usually a name for helicopters that look for injured victims or lost people and rescue them.

Satellite
Usually called Sat Nav, this uses signals from GPS (Global Positioning System) satellites high in space.

Find out more

Websites

http://www.angliacampus.com/education/fire/london/applianc.htm
A look at the many kinds of firefighting vehicles used in London and around England.

http://www.lafire.com/fire_boats/the_boats.htm
One of many sites describing fireboats, how they work and their history, in this case for Los Angeles, USA.

http://www.londonambulance.nhs.uk/aboutus/vehicles/vehicles.html
The vehicles of the London Ambulance Service, the world's largest free-to-use ambulance organisation, which helps an average of three people every minute.

http://www.rnli.org.uk/who_we_are/boats_and_stations
All about Britain's Royal National Lifeboat Institution, including pages on the boats used such as the Trent, Severn and Tamar types.

http://www.angliaone.org.uk/
One of the UK's busiest air ambulance organisations, covering more than one-tenth the area of England.

http://www.wildlandfire.com/pics/air/air.htm
Photos of firefighting planes in action, including the CL-415 Superscooper.

Further reading

Emergency Vehicles (Transportation Around the World) by Chris Oxlade, Heinemann 2007

Emergency Vehicles (QED Machines at Work) by Ian Graham, QED/Quarto 2006

Ambulance Crew, The Police, Firefighters, Rescue at Sea and other titles in the People Who Help Us series by Clare Oliver, Franklin Watts 2007

Fire Engine (Machines at Work), Dorling Kindersley 2006

Note to parents and teachers:
Every effort has been made by the Publishers to ensure that the websites in this book are suitable for children, that they are of the highest educational value, and that they contain no inappropriate or offensive material. However, because of the nature of the Internet, it is impossible to guarantee that the contents of these sites will not be altered. We strongly advise that Internet access is supervised by a responsible adult.

Index